D1173028

BORN FREE FOUNDATION

Lion Rescue

True-Life Stories

Lion Rescue

True-Life Stories

Written by
Sara Starbuck

First edition for the United States published in 2017
by Barron's Educational Series, Inc.

All inquiries should be addressed to:
Barron's Educational Series, Inc.
250 Wireless Boulevard
Hauppauge, New York 11788
www.barronseduc.com

Library of Congress Control Number: 2016950464
ISBN: 978-1-4380-0989-6

Date of Manufacture: January 2017
Manufactured by: RRD Shenzhen, Shenzhen, Guangdong, China

Printed in China
9 8 7 6 5 4 3 2 1

Hello everyone,

At Born Free we believe that every animal deserves the chance to live its life without pain or exploitation.

Our story began when I traveled to Kenya in 1964 to star in a film with my late husband, Bill Travers. *Born Free* (the movie that gave the charity its name) was based on a best-selling book by the naturalist Joy Adamson. It told the remarkable story of Elsa, a lion cub who was orphaned when Joy's husband, George Adamson, was forced to shoot Elsa's mother in self-defense. Elsa was raised almost like a member of the Adamson family. But she was also taught to hunt like a lion, so when the time came, Elsa had the skills she needed to live in the wild.

Joy and George set Elsa free in the Meru National Park, and their story helped to change the way that people thought about lions. The strong bond that Elsa shared with the Adamsons showed that lions should not be considered brutal killers, to be shot and displayed as safari trophies. Elsa became a symbol for the right of all animals to live freely in the wild.

Making the film had a deep and lasting effect on us. Our work with George and Joy, and the lions we met, sparked a lifelong commitment to wildlife and, in 1984, we started our own charity with our eldest son, Will. Since then the Born Free Foundation has grown and grown.

Today, led by Will, our team is devoted to eradicating animal cruelty and suffering around the world. With over a hundred projects, Born Free protects lions, elephants, tigers, gorillas, wolves, polar bears, dolphins, marine turtles, and many more species in their natural habitats, working with local communities to help people and wildlife live together without conflict.

This is the true story of Bella and Simba. I hope you enjoy it.

Virginia McKenna
Actress and Founder Trustee, Born Free Foundation

BORN FREE AROUND THE WORLD

Animal Welfare

Born Free exposes animal suffering and fights cruelty.

Wild Animal Rescue

Born Free develops and supports many wild animal rescue centers.

Canada

United Kingdom

USA

South America

Conservation

Born Free protects wild animals in their natural habitats.

Communities and Education

Born Free works closely with communities who live alongside the projects we support.

Europe

rance • **Romania**

China

India

Africa

Vietnam

Indonesia

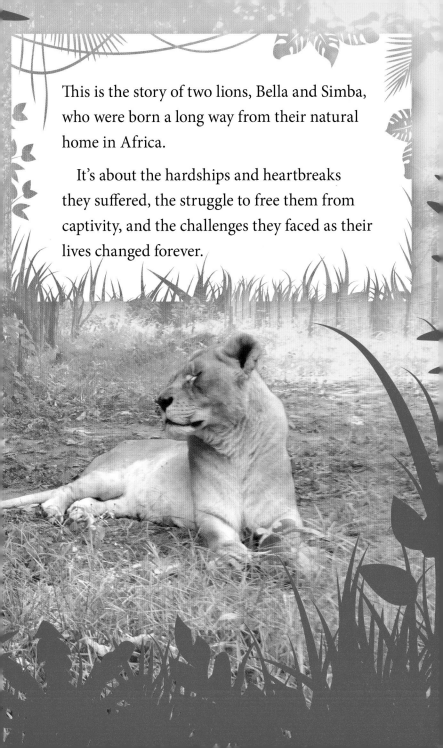

This is the story of two lions, Bella and Simba, who were born a long way from their natural home in Africa.

It's about the hardships and heartbreaks they suffered, the struggle to free them from captivity, and the challenges they faced as their lives changed forever.

Bella

FACTFILE

- Born in Romania
- Grew up in a run-down Romanian zoo
- Hates snow and goat's meat
- Personality—affectionate, playful, and feisty. Loves hanging out with humans
- Favorite toy—a bright orange bowling ball
- Bushpigs annoy her
- Growls at thunder clouds as if they are growling at her
- Loves to eat. Favorite dinner—steak
- Favorite hobby—sunbathing

FACTFILE

Simba

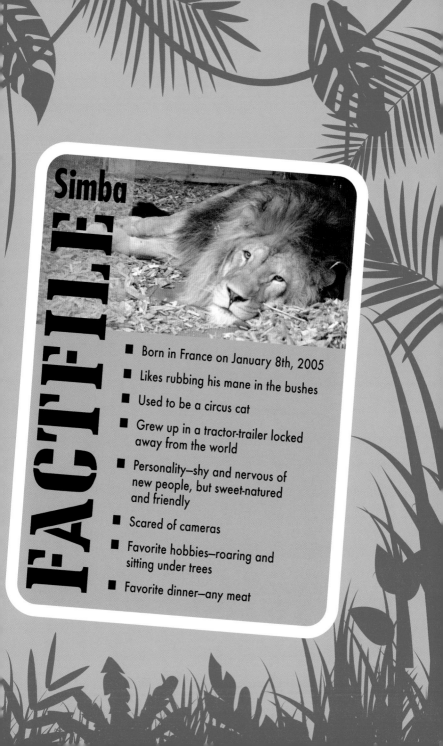

- Born in France on January 8th, 2005
- Likes rubbing his mane in the bushes
- Used to be a circus cat
- Grew up in a tractor-trailer locked away from the world
- Personality—shy and nervous of new people, but sweet-natured and friendly
- Scared of cameras
- Favorite hobbies—roaring and sitting under trees
- Favorite dinner—any meat

Learn a new lion fact
every time you see me.

Chapter One

Bella

December 2006
Buhusi Zoo, Romania

Far away from the sun-baked plains of Africa, on a snowy hillside in Romania, it was feeding time at the Buhusi Zoo. A tired zookeeper cracked open an old freezer and the smell of week-old meat poured out. A hungry rumbling echoed from the open cages. A huge bear rolled toward the rusty bars of her enclosure, snorting great clouds of breath in the frosty air. Chunks of chicken were hauled out of the freezer and piled into a wheelbarrow. The zookeeper sighed, knowing that this morning, like every morning, there would not be enough food.

The keeper gripped the wheelbarrow and pushed through the snow. The bear got her chunk of meat. And the small family of lean dingoes had a portion to fight over.

Then there was Bella. At first, her cage—cramped and bare like the others—seemed empty. But up from the grimy floor rose the outline of a thin lioness with a strangely curved back, and through the swirling snow peered a golden, heart-shaped face with sad, blind eyes. Bella. The lioness with a broken heart.

Once Bella had a mate, a handsome lion named Fuji, and two tiny cubs. Bella's blindness didn't matter to Fuji, and it certainly didn't stop her from being a wonderful mother to her newborns.

FACT FILE

Lion cubs, like human babies, are born quite helpless and are completely dependent on their mothers. In the wild, lionesses will choose a secluded den away from the pride to give birth. They are fiercely protective and will fight to the death for their children. The cubs are hidden in the private den for weeks, safe from hungry predators. They only meet the rest of their pride when their mother knows that they are ready.

She loved to lick and nuzzle them. But in Buhusi, the zookeepers used to take Bella's babies away from her so that they would get used to being handled by humans. This disruptive routine broke the bond between Bella and her cubs. Bella's milk dried up and she was no longer able to feed them. The little cubs became sickly and died.

But this awful loss was just the start of Bella's sadness. Shortly after the death of Bella and Fuji's second cub, Fuji fell ill, too. He had a kidney infection. With the attention of a vet, it wouldn't have been that serious, but it was left untreated. Fuji grew weaker and weaker and Bella never left his side. Finally, one night, Fuji died.

After losing her family, Bella became desperate for human company. Most cats walk alone, but lions are different. They are sociable and spend their lives living among their extended families. As the zookeepers watched Bella curl up against the cold in her empty cage, they began to worry that the last of their big cats would waste away and die from loneliness.

Chapter Two
Simba

August 2010
Vernay, Southern France

Far from the chilly hills of Buhusi, by the side of a road in France, a shaggy-maned lion was sprawled in his trailer, panting in the heat. He had no water to drink. In Africa, he would have been looped over the low branches of a jackalberry tree, or hiding in the tall savanna grass. But not here, towed from town to town, with nothing to do but wait for nightfall.

From the distance, the lion looked like a fallen king, bedraggled and miserable, but still mighty to behold. And he had a name to match, Simba.

A group of children spotted Simba on the roadside and approached his trailer, nervously. They danced around the bars, taunting him, trying to make him roar. If he had, they would have scattered like crows from a farmer's gun.

Lions start roaring from about one year old and often roar at night.

But Simba was unimpressed. He stared at the children lazily and turned his back, showing hindquarters as smooth and muscled as cast bronze. Then he yawned, and nestled down again, his massive head resting on his paws. It was a good thing for Simba that lions like to snooze for about twenty hours of every day. With nothing else to do, and only the cramped quarters of the beast wagon to pace back and forth in, he would have gone out of his mind with boredom.

It's not that Simba was pining for the wild. The beast wagon was the only real home he had known. He had been given to the animal trainer by a zoo when he was just a few months old. Since then, the tiny trailer was the only space he'd had, except for a small exercise run that his owner sometimes attached to the side of his cage. And even that was hardly enough room for a majestic animal like Simba to stretch his legs properly.

A lion can run up to 40 miles per hour for short distances. In the wild, their territory might cover 100 square miles. That's about as large as 48,000 football fields.

FACT FILE

Apart from his trainer, her husband, and the occasional gang of curious kids, Simba was alone. He had never known kindness or respect, and he never had other lions to play with or learn from.

By the age of two, a wild lion has been hunting alongside its parents for more than a year. It can bring down a gazelle all by itself.

FACT FILE

Simba hadn't learned any of the survival skills that would have been vital on the African savanna. In the wild, he wouldn't have lasted a week.

Chapter Three
Bella

February 2007
Buhusi Zoo, Romania

An eerie silence had fallen over Buhusi Zoo. Most of the animals were gone now, and the bitter winter wind whistled through the empty cages and rattled their rusty iron bars. Romanian winters are always cold. Perfect weather for a snow leopard, perhaps, but for its distant cousin the African lion, it was a miserable time of year. Bella should have been lying in the sun, watching the wildebeests sweeping by, or nudging aside a pink-bellied hippo to find a place at the waterhole. Instead, she was hiding away in a corner of her tiny pen, huddled in a dark concrete cage. But things were about to change.

In 2003, a group of charity workers called The Lion's Roar Project had begun working to improve Buhusi Zoo. They had some success, but when the zoo closed in 2007, their mission changed. With help from Born Free and other organizations, they set about finding new homes for as many of Buhusi's animals as possible. It was a tough task, and poor Bella was still waiting.

Born Free wanted Bella to be rehomed at the Shamwari Game Reserve in South Africa where two lions from her pride had already been sent. But Bella's vet was worried about her left eye, which was swollen with the painful disease Glaucoma. The slightest knock could have caused it to start bleeding. And with the vision in her right eye already clouded, they didn't want to risk blinding her completely. Poor Bella had problems with her skeleton too, after so long in such poor conditions. She was simply in too sick and sorry a state to be moved very far at all.

Nobody knows much about Bella's life before she arrived at Buhusi Zoo, but it's likely that for all of the zoo's problems, it was still better than where she started. As a cub, Bella was probably used as a prop by Black Sea photographers, who would charge tourists to have their photo taken with her. She would have been taken from her mother at a very early age, kept on a chain, and reared on cow's milk, which doesn't have enough essential vitamins or protein for a growing lion.

Without the nourishing milk she needed, Bella grew up with deformed back legs and a damaged spine. She would never be able to walk properly. Once Bella was too big to look cute for the photographer's snaps, she was dumped at a zoo to breed the next generation of captive lions. There was nothing happy to look forward to in Bella's life. At least, there hadn't been.

Chapter Four

Simba

August, 2012
Vernay, Southern France

In a garden in the South of France, everything was quiet and still. A big male rabbit was sitting by a patch of brambles, twitching his nose and listening for trouble. But not closely enough! With a huge crash, Simba threw himself against the bars of his beast wagon, lunging for the rabbit with his massive paws. He may have been born in captivity, and never had the chance to kill his own meal, but the instinct to hunt and feed was still in him. On the inside, Simba was as wild as ever.

Lions' bodies are built for hunting. They are ambush predators. They don't have stamina for a long chase and their prey are some of the fastest animals on the planet. The lionesses usually do most of the hunting and work as a team, while the male lions' job is to protect the pride and the territory.

No one can truly know what happened to Simba while he lived with the circus trainers. Trainers are not supposed to bully or hurt their animals, but there are plenty that still do and a circus ring is far from a lion's natural habitat. What we do know for sure is that things were bad for Simba by the time he reached Vernay. At least at the circus there would have been other animals and sights and sounds to keep Simba occupied. Here, there was nothing but the odd bunny to frighten.

Lions like to talk to each other. As well as roaring, they make other sounds such as grunts and hissing noises.

FACT FILE

Simba's trainer was no better at business than she was at keeping lions. Eventually, she struggled to make enough money to look after herself, let alone Simba, and when things got tough, she gave up on lion taming altogether. Simba's trailer was moved into the back garden. When she let him into his exercise compound, he often refused to go back into the beast wagon altogether. Sometimes he would be left out there all night, roaring at the moon and growling at

the shadows. But the enclosure wasn't secure enough to house a full grown lion in his prime. If Simba had managed to get out, it would have been terrible.

By their very nature, lions are dangerous animals, even one as shy and gentle as Simba. Locked away all the time, isolated from the rest of the world and with no opportunity to indulge his wild instincts, the young lion was a ticking time bomb.

Perhaps some part of Simba understood that life should have been better, because he fell into deep despair. The sound of his lonely roars at night—not to mention the threat of escape—was too much for his human neighbors to bear. A phone call was made to Fondation 30 Millions d'Amis, a French organization, who rescue unhappy wild animals in captivity. They alerted the French authorities and the young lion's suffering was brought to their attention. One way or another, the world Simba knew was about to change.

Chapter Five
Bella

October, 2008
Brasov Zoo, Romania

There was a storm coming. Thundery black clouds were gathering in the skies above Buhusi Zoo. In the distance, lightning fuzzed and crackled, whipping across the mountains like a crazy science experiment.

Bella had been moved to Brasov Zoo. It was only two hours away, but it couldn't have been more different. It gave Bella a safe home while she had surgery to save the sight in her good eye, and a comfortable place to recover.

At the end of 2008, the Born Free Foundation's veterinary consultant, John Knight, specialist veterinary surgeon, Dr. David Donaldson, and a team of Romanian vets performed Bella's long-overdue operation and removed her diseased left eye. The operation took place in the Kronvet Clinic—an ordinary vet's practice in Brasov—which offered the use of their staff and facilities. They had an anesthetic machine, usually used for cats and dogs, but which could be adapted to the much larger task of keeping a lion asleep during an operation.

The surgery went without a hitch and Bella made a speedy recovery. She was given supplements for her arthritis, worming medicine, and vaccinations against rabies and tetanus. She even had a pedicure to make sure her formidable claws were in tip-top condition.

FACT FILE

A lion's claws grow as a series of layers. They sharpen their claws by scratching trees to keep them extra pointy.

A couple of months after her first surgery, the veterinary team reassembled at Brasov, and Bella underwent a second operation to remove the cataract in her otherwise healthy right eye. The veterinary team at Brasov were very pleased. There were no complications and everyone was hoping that the removal of the cataract would give her some long-distance vision.

The storm working its way toward the abandoned Buhusi Zoo never broke. Instead, it swept onward, over the mountains and on to Brasov. A blanket of thick black clouds blocked out the afternoon light and the rain soaked every surface. But throughout all the excitement of the storm, Bella was out for the count in her own cozy, heated enclosure.

The lioness seemed happy in her temporary home. Her fluffy, white tummy rose and fell steadily as she slept off the effects of the anesthetic. Since arriving at Brasov, Bella had developed a taste for steak and it showed in her healthy coat and swelling belly. In fact, the zoo's vet, Dr. Ion Brumar, had said that she would have to be put on a diet if she got any fatter. What a turnaround for Bella. Only a year earlier, she had grown so thin that there was barely any lion left at all.

When lions manage to catch their prey, they will feast on it until they're completely stuffed. Lions are carnivores, and they will eat any meat they can lay their paws on. Their back teeth, which are called carnassials, work like a pair of scissors and come in handy when tackling tough, fresh meat.

Even a lion's tongue, with its tiny barbed spines (just like a pet cat's), is designed for scraping meat from bones.

Chapter Six
Simba

October 2012
Vernay, Southern France

Asleep in his rusty prison, Simba was having a nightmare. His muscled body twitched and flinched as if he was trying to get away from something terrible. His musty smell filled the tiny trailer and ticks and fleas wove their way in and out of his huge, matted scruff of mane.

Simba was in his prime, or at least he should have been. He had paws the size of loaves of bread and an impressive mane, which would have served him well in the wild.

At seven, Simba would have left his mother's pride long ago. He would have traveled beyond the safety of his birth territory and become a trespasser in enemy land. If he survived long enough to find a promising new area, the next step would have been for him to take over another pride. But, of course, the resident males wouldn't just roll over for a new boss.

Just as Simba started to doze off again, his sensitive nose caught a whiff of something new and intriguing on the breeze. There were people nearby, and getting closer. He rose to his feet, sniffing curiously at the air. The smell was getting stronger. They were coming straight for him, calling out his name, four men with bags and notebooks and faces that were a picture of kindness and concern.

Simba's trainer was there, too, standing awkwardly at the edge of the group, with her eyes lowered and her arms crossed. The strangers were asking her questions and scribbling down her muttered answers with great interest. Something was up. Something was about to change.

Chapter Seven
Bella

February, 2009
Brasov Zoo, Romania

Bella lay on her back with her paws in the air. She was exhausted and happy. She stared up at the clouds and watched intently as a plane vanished behind them, leaving a long white trail in its wake. The sky was a busy place and Bella didn't want to miss any of the excitement. Before her surgery, she never had much of a reason to look up. She wouldn't have seen the stars at night, or the reds and golds of sunset, or the birds in flight. For years, everything had been a complete blur. Now, at last, the world was coming into focus.

The second operation to remove Bella's cataract had been a success. Her single eye was much better, with vastly improved long-distance vision, though she still had trouble seeing things close-up. Sometimes she would pace her enclosure extra slowly, carefully picking her way through the long grass and the bushes as if she was measuring out the space. In fact, it was because she couldn't see where she was putting her feet or what she was about to walk through until it was right under her nose. But when something captured her attention from a distance, she would bound toward it confidently, her hunter's instincts taking over.

Brasov was just a stopping point on Bella's journey. The plans were well underway for her move to Lilongwe, and the mountains of paperwork needed to move a lioness around the world were finally out of the way, too. It wouldn't be much longer before Bella could exchange the Romanian snow for the endless sunshine of Malawi.

Bella's body suddenly tensed as she sniffed the air. She froze, not twitching a muscle. Only her tail betrayed her agitation.

FACT FILE

The lion's tail is the only one in the cat family with a tassel at the tip. The tail is very important for balance. Females use their raised tail as a "follow me" signal for the cubs. They also use it to signal each other during a group hunt.

Bella's target, Oscar, was the other lion at the Brasov Zoo who had recently been moved into Bella's enclosure. As Bella was half-blind and had such a weak spine and back legs, a more powerfully built lion like Oscar might have harmed her. As it turned out, even though Oscar was young and stronger, Bella kept him firmly in his place. Bella was the dominant lion and even though she had been bitterly lonely after losing Fuji and her cubs, she didn't want Oscar anywhere near her. Oscar didn't dare approach her, unless she was lying down, and then he would quietly lie down too, at a respectful distance.

Chapter Eight
Simba

November 2012
The NHC (Natuurhulpcentrum Sanctuary), Belgium

Simba sat on a high wooden platform in his new grassy enclosure. The sun dazzled in Simba's glittering golden eyes, but he didn't move a muscle. His front paws dangled lazily over the edge of the platform but his black-tipped ears were cocked inquisitively. It may not have looked as if he was doing much but, in fact, Simba was quite busy. He was alert and wide awake, listening to the morning. The Belgian wildlife rescue center was full of people and animals bustling about as the day began. After spending the past seven years alone in a trailer, Simba's superb senses must have been going haywire.

A lion can hear the call of its prey or the roar of another pride member from a mile away, and their rotating ears can pinpoint the direction of every sound. Their sense of smell is so sharp that not only can they tell if prey is nearby, but also if it has come and gone, and how long ago.

By day, lions don't see the world much differently from us. But at night, it's a different story. Once the sun goes down, a lion's sense of sight is six times more effective than a human's. The lion's eye is wonderfully adapted to pick up and magnify even the tiniest amount of light from the moon and stars. They have large, round pupils to catch as much light as possible, quite different from the vertical slits of a house cat's eyes. Even their faces help their night vision. The white strips of fur under their eyes reflect faint light, bouncing it directly into their eyes to maximize their sight.

The people who had turned up for Simba that day in Vernay were from the Fondation 30 Million D'Amis. They had come to take Simba away from his very relieved trainer. He was moved to the Natuurhulpcentrum (the NHC) in Belgium, a wildlife center that takes in animals who are sick or in need of help. It wasn't a permanent home for Simba, but it was a fantastic start.

Because he had spent so much of his life locked away in a cramped metal cage, Simba didn't really know what to make of his little patch of freedom, and he didn't trust the new humans—the center's friendly keepers—who all seemed to know his name.

Like all cats, lions need shadowy, concealed places where they can feel safe. In the wild, a lion will seek out a well-positioned den or hiding spot when they're scared, stalking prey, or sometimes just to get away from it all and enjoy some peace and quiet.

FACT FILE

But cats are also curious, and after a while, the commotion outside became too much for Simba to resist. First, he had stuck his head out from his dark enclosure and sniffed the clean, fresh air. His mane looked like a giant dandelion blowing around in the wind. Then there was a paw, one big pad testing the ground beyond the short tunnel that led outside. Then another paw. Then suddenly, Simba was outside, running and rolling about and exploring his spacious new home. It was probably the first time he'd ever had fun in his life.

After a month at the NHC, Simba was still nervous around strangers, but he quickly got used to his new keepers and Bart Hilven was a clear favorite. As Bart approached from a distance, humming a tune to himself, Simba raised his head at once.

His handsome face was as unreadable as the sphinx, but his tail swished around madly, betraying his curiosity. He yawned luxuriously, exposing a cave full of fangs and a huge, rolling pink tongue. Then he got to his feet and stretched his body.

Bart was just passing, but he stopped to say hello. Simba slunk down from his platform and swaggered over to meet him. He pushed his nose between the bars to sniff Bart's hand, then rubbed his face on it, affectionately.

FACT FILE

Lions will rub each other in greeting. This rubbing can be quite vigorous and forceful. Males will sometimes knock each other over. This rubbing serves a purpose. There are scent glands on the corner of lions' mouths. Rubbing deposits this scent on the other lion. This scent is like a mark of bonding or ownership.

It was obvious that Simba was so much happier now, but he was still a very long way from Africa.

Chapter Nine
Bella

February 2009
On the way to Malawi

Finally the day came for Bella to leave Romania. It was snowing again—the last snow the big cat would ever see! Bella never liked the snow and she certainly wasn't going to miss it on the sun-baked plains of Malawi. As evening drew on and the light faded, Born Free's expert vet, John Knight, darted Bella with a sedative so she could be loaded safely into her travel container.

While she snoozed, the rescue team lifted Bella gently onto a stretcher and loaded her into her traveling crate, then onto the back of a waiting truck. The Romanian press were there, scribbling notes and jostling for position around Bella's crate. After months of fundraising, Bella had become a celebrity, and people from all over the world wanted to share her journey from heartache to happiness.

When Bella was woken up for the journey, she wasn't at all bothered by all of the people buzzing around or the flash of camera bulbs. She handled everything, dozy as she was, in true

celebrity style. Soon the truck was rumbling through the gates of the zoo and off toward the mountainous road to Bucharest. The next time Bella's paws touched land it would be the sandy red soil of Africa.

From Bucharest, Bella was flown to Heathrow Airport where even more journalists had gathered, hoping to catch a glimpse of the famous one-eyed lioness. In the huge shadow of a Kenya Airways jet, Virginia McKenna was waiting to meet her. She would be accompanying the Born Free team on the last leg of their journey to Malawi.

It was a long but uneventful flight. Finally, Bella and her team were greeted at Lilongwe Airport by Lee Stewart, the smiling manager of the Wildlife Centre, along with the other members of his team. A huge tree-filled enclosure was waiting for the sanctuary's very first lion. Everything had been carefully considered, from making sure her resting platforms weren't too high off the ground for her to reach with her damaged spine, to building a spacious indoor house where she could hide away from people and shelter from the sudden, heavy downpours that drenched the land during the rainy season. It was absolutely perfect. All that had been missing was Bella.

Chapter Ten
Simba

December 2012
NHC

The telephone had been ringing off the hook in the main office, but with all of NHC's volunteers busy, the answer machine had to pick up the slack. Fifteen new animals had been rescued and admitted already and it wasn't yet lunchtime. In the operating room, a vet was desperately trying to save the life of a fox cub with the puncture marks of a nasty fight on his tummy and a shredded left ear.

Simba was busy hunting pigeon. The unfortunate bird had no idea that she had chosen to land in a lion pen. She was too busy preening her gray feathers to notice Simba creeping up stealthily. Soon Simba was in striking distance of his prey. The pigeon hadn't spotted a thing. Simba crouched, holding his breath, waiting for the right moment . . . Then he pounced! Freshly preened feathers puffed into the air and settled on the ground as the bird was crushed in Simba's awesome jaws.

FACT FILE

Lions have several hunting methods. They might stalk their prey slowly with a final burst of speed at the end. Or sometimes they lie in wait where they are sure to find prey—often near water.

Simba's killer instinct had truly kicked in, and his interest in stalking and hunting had soared. He wasn't exactly an experienced hunter, though, and after having caught his prize, he wasn't quite sure what to do with it next. It didn't look like his normal food. The bird's body hung limply from his mouth. Its feathers were tickling his nose. This was all new for Simba and more than a little confusing.

The NHC had already successfully rehomed five captive lions to Africa and the team there were all hoping that Simba would be the sixth. Unfortunately, there aren't many people with the right space to house a full-grown male lion. So while calls were made and people scurried around Simba would have to wait where he was. Of course, that was no bad thing. It was paradise compared to the squalor of his old home and he was getting the best possible care. His muscles were growing stronger every day. Simba was king of the wildlife center. All he needed now was a friend to share his kingdom with. The NHC's phone was ringing again. This time it was someone from Born Free's UK office inquiring about Simba. They were looking for a potential mate for a female lion living in Africa and wanted to know more about him.

It was turning out to be a big day for Simba. First a successful pigeon hunt and now this—a potential mate, and maybe even a new permanent home in Africa! Of course, he knew nothing about the telephone call, but behind the scenes, things were starting to move fast.

Chapter Eleven
Bella

March 2009
Lilongwe, Malawi

Lilongwe Wildlife Centre sprawls between the old
town and the modern city center of Malawi's capital,
just off the busy Kenyatta Road. It was set up in 2007
and provides sanctuary space for rescued, confiscated,
orphaned, and injured wild animals of many species.
Over 400 acres of beautiful, natural landscape,
as close to the wilderness as a sanctuary can be.
And there, in the middle, was two acres, carefully
cordoned off by 1,300 ft (400 m) of strong fencing,
that now belonged entirely to Bella.

The truck with the Centre's newest arrival pulled to a halt, and the Born Free team began to unload Bella's crate. In a few short minutes, the job was done and the excited workers were ready to throw the bolts and open the door to Bella's new life.

Bella didn't want to come out at first. In typical cat fashion, she did the precise opposite of what everyone else wanted. She sat in her traveling crate, not budging an inch. Beyond the open doorway lay two acres of beautiful enclosure, but Bella stayed exactly where she was, her back to the glorious view. There were so many new people to take in and so many unfamiliar scents in the air that she was feeling quite overwhelmed. Better to remain in the safety of her small, familiar crate.

Nearly an hour later, Bella started to show signs that she might be ready to come out. Her one good eye blinked in the bright sun and she lifted a paw cautiously beyond the threshold of the heavy metal box.

Lions are digitigrade walkers. This means they walk on their toes. Each paw has a soft pad to make its movements quiet.

Bella stood still and sniffed the air. Romania had smelled of pine trees and sometimes spring flowers. Now, there was the heady aroma of tall grass and a crisp note from the waterhole that had been built especially for her. There was the musty smell

of other animals—though Bella was no stranger to that—and with it the dry African dust.

There were new sounds, too. The chatter of baboons, a snake sliding through a patch of lemon grass, and the rustling of a vulture's feathers as it flapped overhead. Everything was different. Even the sun was brighter and hotter than Bella had ever known. After a few minutes of looking around and carefully taking everything in, she finally stepped out of the crate. With her head held high and her face alert, Bella the African lion stood for the first time in her life on African soil.

Bella stood on the dusty scrubland staring at a tangle of Chilema trees, swinging her head left and right to check out the handful of people standing quietly along the fence line, watching her. And then, unexpectedly, something quite special happened. Bella walked over to Virginia McKenna, quite purposefully, and fixed her with a one-eyed stare. She held her gaze for a long time. It was as if she knew who Virginia was and she wanted to say thank you. Perhaps Bella could sense the love that Virginia McKenna had for lions, or perhaps it was her long-sightedness, making her strain to focus on the nearest of the human figures. But for everyone present, it was a touching moment; a lioness and a woman, standing together, looking at each other with respect and friendship.

Lions have a cuddly side and can be very affectionate with each other. When they are raised in captivity, they often develop deep bonds with the people who look after them.

FACT FILE

At last, Bella broke the spell and walked steadily toward the cover of the trees. Now, in the orange glow of the late afternoon sun, her coat was the very same color as the golden, knee-high grass that she waded through. The perfect hunter's camouflage for an African big cat.

With a final backward glance over her shoulder at Virginia, Bella melted into the long grass and was gone. Free at last to run and prowl and climb and explore her new home.

Chapter Twelve
Simba

February 2014
On the way to Malawi

Born Free thought that gentle Simba would be the perfect match for their lonely lioness, Bella. By now, Bella had been living at Lilongwe for five years. She'd become a poster-cat for the sanctuary. Visitors adored her because they usually got to see Bella up close. She was loved and she was happy, but there was still a cat-shaped space beside her.

Meanwhile, Simba was now nine years old and still hadn't ever really known another lion. He still hadn't run as fast as he could or felt the hot African sun on his back. His lonely roars at night had never been answered.

Both lions had been without a companion for too long and that needed to change. So the Born Free Foundation, together with the NHC and the Lilongwe Wildlife Centre, began working to bring them together.

Lions are all different. The spots above their muzzle make a unique pattern.

Moving a full grown lion to another country 5,000 miles (8,000 km) away takes a lot of planning, but after months of fundraising, preparation, and paperwork on both sides of the ocean, Simba was finally ready to make the journey from Europe to the heart of Africa.

It's risky to transport a lion for more than 24 hours, as they can get dehydrated and antsy, so every step of the journey had to be carefully considered. Bart, Simba's keeper, had even been rehearsing how he would lure

Simba into the traveling crate for months before the Big Day—using a few big chunks of steak.

Then, early one drizzly February morning, the Born Free relocation team arrived at the NHC. They traveled in a convoy of six shiny Land Rovers, like knights rescuing a strange, hairy princess. One of them, decorated with paw prints, was towing a bright red horse-trailer fit for a lion. It was time to start the epic journey to the Lilongwe Wildlife Centre. Simba would be moving into an enclosure right next door to Bella's. A big crowd had gathered to say goodbye to Simba. Everyone at the NHC was going to miss their giant, sweet-natured

sanctuary-cat, especially Bart. The local press were there too, taking lots of photos, but Simba wasn't a natural celebrity like Bella. He was

camera shy and the jostle of staring humans made him uncomfortable.

The team got to work as quickly as possible. Bart coaxed Simba into the traveling crate using steak, which worked perfectly. All those weeks of practicing

had paid off. Once the doors were shut and firmly bolted behind him, Simba calmly settled in a comfy spot, happy to go along with things. Of course, Bart would be going on the journey too, to keep an eye on him along the way.

Finally, the convoy of Land Rovers pulled away from the center. Anyone who saw them would have assumed they were transporting a rock star or royalty, perhaps even a diplomat. Although, if the careful pace hadn't given them away, the lead Land Rover, emblazoned with the Born Free insignia and painted with its lion paw prints, might have. Simba and his entourage were escorted proudly and securely on the four-hour journey to Amsterdam's Schiphol Airport. It was a parade fit for a king.

On arrival at Schipol, Simba was received by the ground team of Kenya Airways. Born Free was Kenya Airways' chosen charity, and along with collecting for them inflight they had agreed to help Born Free with their rescue missions by transporting the animals free of charge. Which meant animals like Simba could be flown to their new homes on faraway shores.

While Simba waited in quarantine, the paperwork was dealt with and the crate was securely strapped onto a pallet ready for loading onto the plane. Simba's flight to Malawi was to have a short touchdown in Nairobi's Jomo Kenyatta Airport. Then they would fly across Zambia and onto Lilongwe.

At Nairobi, Virginia McKenna would be joining the team for the final leg of the journey. It was the eve of the Born Free Foundation's 30th Anniversary, which made the timing of Simba's return to Africa even more perfect.

Chapter Thirteen
Bella

February 2014
Lilongwe

In the heat of the African sun, the grasslands of Malawi shimmered like gold. A cloudless blue sky stretched out forever, and the earth was cracked and thirsty.

On a small patch of the dry soil, under the shady branches of an acacia tree, Bella was playing with her new toy; a stuffed sack covered in antelope poop. It had been left for her to find in her enclosure that morning and since discovering it, Bella had dragged it around with her everywhere. The sack was filled with straw and leaves and smeared with the droppings of one of her prey animals, as well as a dash of catnip spray and a drop of lavender oil, all which smelled absolutely wonderful to Bella.

The team at Lilongwe had tried their hardest to make sure their resident lioness was happy and comfortable. Interesting toys had been left all over Bella's enclosure to encourage her to get to know every inch of her home.

Limited eyesight had made Bella a little reluctant to leave the corners she quickly familiarized herself with, so once a week, blood-flavored ice pops filled with lion treats had been left in the unexplored reaches of her enclosure. This was done to tempt her in new directions, as well as to cool her down in the afternoon heat. And the program worked. Slowly but surely, Bella had started to roam more freely around her enclosure as she sniffed out her new playthings.

Some of Bella's old habits were deep-rooted. She still loved human company, for example. If someone approached, she would rush over eagerly and welcome them by rubbing along her fence, purring and whuffing friendly greetings at them.

If she was feeling particularly excitable, she might jump around happily, scratching the ground and pushing against the fence. At other times, she would roll onto her back at the foot of the fence, with her feet flopping around.

But Bella was certainly no pushover. When bushpigs came sniffing around interrupting her human visits, Bella would quickly chase them off, running alongside them on the other side of the fence and snarling ferociously. Occasionally, she would stalk the keepers as they cleaned out her stall or checked the fencing around her enclosure. Thankfully, she had no interest in eating her human helpers. It was all fun and games for Bella.

As it was the beginning of the rainy season in Malawi, thick gray clouds swept in quickly. The air felt hot and heavy.

The smell of wet earth carried in on the wind and Bella stood to sniff the air. The first drop of rain fell with a heavy splash and you could almost hear the bone dry soil sigh with relief. In the cold of Romania, Bella had always hidden away from storms, but not here in Malawi. The thunder boomed and Bella stood firm, growling at the clouds. Then the monsoon rain began in earnest.

The staff at the Lilongwe Wildlife Sanctuary were buzzing with excitement. It was a big day for them; they had another new lion arriving.

Jonathan Vaughan, who was now the center manager, had been up since 5 A.M. making preparations for the newcomer.

Everyone had hoped that the sun would be shining to welcome their latest resident, but after four days of unbroken blue skies it was now raining hard.

Bella watched all the comings and goings curiously. Her almond-shaped, amber eye took in the staff and volunteers dashing urgently from place to place. Nobody seemed to have any time to stop and say hello, and it was very unusual these days for Bella to find herself ignored.

She sat in silence, flicking away flies with her tail. They were a constant nuisance, nibbling the edges of her ears and tickling her whiskers, but a few squirts of citronella repellent from the keepers usually did the trick and kept them away.

In fact, Bella loved being sprayed with it. But today the biting, tickling flies weren't going away, and there still wasn't a keeper around to help.

In fact, a clever volunteer had already come up with a nifty solution to the problem, hanging an old broom head on the mesh of the enclosure that Bella could use to scratch away the flies on her face. Unfortunately, Bella had her own ideas about how best to use the broom. She'd been gnawing on it like a toothbrush.

Meanwhile, the perimeters of the new lion's enclosure were being given a last look. It wouldn't be long now before Bella's neighbor-to-be arrived. But if they expected her to be polite and friendly, someone was going to have come up with some breakfast.

Chapter Fourteen
Simba

February 2014
Malawi

When Simba jetted in to Africa, he received a hero's welcome. Everyone was eager to see how the famous lion was doing on his epic journey. Simba behaved beautifully, even when the vet gave him a quick examination.

The first people off the plane were the experts from Born Free. Everyone was weary after their long journey, but they were overjoyed to see the welcome committee with their colorful banner. There were hugs and handshakes all around, then it was time to get Simba back on solid ground again.

When the airport staff realized that a special cargo had arrived, they gathered around too, hoping to sneak a look at the "mkango"—the lion—arriving home from exile in the cold North. The security men held everyone back from Simba's crate, helped by a protective Virginia, reminding everyone in the crowd that Simba needed space so that he didn't become scared.

The journalists' questions were answered as quickly as possible because the team were eager to get Simba to the wildlife center without delay. He was a little more dehydrated after his travels than anyone had expected, and there was still a way to go by road before everyone could relax.

But even though the skies had cleared up by the time Simba had landed in Lilongwe, the morning's heavy rain meant that the narrow roads leading to his new enclosure were dangerously muddy. The truck they had planned to use would never get through.

Luckily, Born Free knew some very helpful people and had organized monsoon-proof transport well in advance. Land Rover had agreed to help out with the rescue, and three sturdy, four-wheeled-drive vehicles had been dispatched from the nearest dealer in Lusaka, capital

of the neighboring country of Zambia. They were driven all the way across Zambia to Malawi, ready to meet Simba and his entourage by the doors of their Kenya Airways jet.

As Team Simba drove in comfort away from the airport, the sky darkened with more rain clouds and, despite their powerful transport, everyone hoped the weather wouldn't get any worse. The land

stretched all around them, a vast scrubland bobbled with rocky green woods. Simba, safe in his trailer, must have inhaled the warm, humid air carrying thousands of exotic new smells to his sensitive nose.

It took eight of Lilongwe's strongest staff to carry Simba's half-ton crate the final few yards to his enclosure. Bart was on hand to offer reassurance and water, and Virginia also stayed with them every step of the way.

Twenty-six hours after leaving Belgium, Simba was carried straight to his night room to be checked over by the veterinary team. Then, as soon as the front of the crate was lifted, Simba rushed straight out. He was looking surprisingly

happy and confident after his long journey. After a
quick snack of a chicken—served whole and crunched
up in no time—it was time for Simba to explore
his new enclosure; an acre of natural forest where
he could run, climb, play, and snooze in the sun. It
was Simba's very own little piece of Africa. Staff and
guests alike had all gathered to watch Simba step
onto the grass for the very first time. The choir from
the entrance had reassembled, too. Accompanied by
African drummers, they began to sing, their voices
rising in harmony to the rhythm of the drums as they
celebrated Simba's arrival.

Simba slipped into the sunlight
and blinked with
amazement as he took

everything in. It was like nothing he had ever experienced before. There was so much space! His new home stretched so far that he couldn't even see where his territory ended. Simba had never had the chance to climb a tree before, but now he was surrounded by them. This was a natural adventure playground, as well as a place of shade and shelter. And what was that, just lying in the road? Another chicken to munch on? Oh yes! This place would do very nicely!

As Simba padded from spot to spot, exploring every inch of his new world, the choir's voices rang out in the bright sunlight that followed the rains. Everything was new for Simba, the tall grass, the hot air, the trees . . . . There was something else, too, a particularly exciting new smell. He wandered over toward the night room next to his. That's where it was coming from, but what was it? It was sort of familiar. He'd have to investigate further, but for now there was too much to see and do.

Simba stood for a moment, his head held high, surveying his new kingdom with unblinking golden eyes. Then he threw back his head, contracted the muscles of his belly and let out an earth-shaking roar. It was deep and powerful; a roar that said "I am here and I'm not to be messed with. And this land? This land is mine."

A king had come home.

Chapter Fifteen
Bella & Simba

Lilongwe,
Malawi

It wasn't exactly love at first sight for Bella and Simba. In fact, after Simba's arrival at Lilongwe, the pair weren't allowed to see each other at all for nearly a month. Simba had to stay quarantined for 30 days while the wildlife center's vets made sure he was in perfect health. A wooden partition was put up between the two lions' night rooms, so that neither of them would be disturbed by the stranger prowling around next door.

They could both smell and hear plenty, though, and Bella was particularly excited about her new neighbor.

She trotted up and down the fence line of her enclosure, purring eagerly. Simba was much more interested in discovering his new surroundings. He had no idea who it was on the other side of the fence making funny noises at him, but over on his side everything was awesome! He was keen to lay claim to every bit of it.

Late one night, after the wooden partition had been taken down, Simba sat by the fence listening to Bella's calls intently, and decided to call back. His roar started low as he worked up to full volume, then it grew and grew, getting deeper and louder until it felt like the ground beneath him was vibrating.

Then something wonderful happened. Bella roared back, then padded over to the fence and sat down, only a few feet from Simba, divided by the chain link fence. Simba hunkered down in the grass and growled. Back and forth, their gruff voices cried out in the darkening night. Simba inched forward so that his paws were touching the fence. He'd never had another lion to talk to before and he liked it.

After a few weeks of neighborly roaring through the fence that divided them, the day came for Bella and Simba to try sharing the same space. The team at Lilongwe, assisted by Tony Wiles, Born Free's Big Cat Specialist, waited nervously, fire extinguishers ready. Bringing solitary lions together is a dangerous business and nobody was sure how they would react when they came face to face. If Bella and Simba started fighting, one or both of them could be injured or even killed.

With their fingers crossed and their hearts thumping in their chests, the Lilongwe staff threw open the gate that divided Simba and Bella's night rooms and Simba sauntered up to greet her. Bella went crazy. Despite all those promising purrs, she was furious to have her territory invaded by this presumptuous young male. She launched into a vicious attack, snarling and lashing out with her powerful claws, then leaping at poor Simba to bite his throat. If it hadn't been for that thick, protective mane of his, she might have broken his neck. Simba roared and backed away, desperate to escape. But Bella kept coming, an angry blur of teeth and claws. Then, just as suddenly as she had lunged, she stopped her frenzied attack and turned away.

Simba slunk off to find a spot to nurse his scratches, as far away as possible. Bella followed him and delivered a few more vicious swipes. Simba didn't know what he'd done wrong. He tried to stay out of Bella's way, but she wouldn't let him rest. Eventually, the team led him back to the safety of his own night room and closed the gate for the night. They'd have to try again tomorrow.

Nobody expected an easy ride. It had always been unlikely that the two lonely lions would bond right away. But as the days went by, the Lilongwe team hoped for a change in Bella's hostile mood. Simba had started hiding away from her as much as possible, and who could blame him? If the pair were ever going to be friends, something would have to be done. And soon.

The problem was Bella. After so long in solitude, her initial curiosity had turned to defensiveness and all those purrs had become threatening snarls. Perhaps her limited vision left her feeling vulnerable and she wanted to show Simba—half her age, more than twice her size—that she was no pushover. It's what she had done with Oscar too. Whatever her reasons, it was working. Simba was truly intimidated.

In desperation, the Lilongwe team tried taking a different approach. Instead of releasing Simba into Bella's territory, they  first let him out into his own space, then allowed Bella to wander across from her own enclosure. To everybody's surprise and delight, it did the trick!

On the foreign soil of Simba's territory, Bella actually started being nice to him. To Simba, this was almost as unnerving as being attacked. His visitor was rolling around on the ground in front of him, and even trying to lick him. What was he supposed to do? Was she going to wallop him again? Unsure how to take this sudden change of mood, Simba slunk back to his night room and sat there, confused, refusing to come out.

It was a start, though, and the center's team were quick to build on it. As the days turned into weeks, the lions were slowly brought together more and more until they began to relax in each other's company. By springtime, they were relaxing in the sun together. By summer, they were trotting around the enclosure in perfect step with each other, and napping in a big furry heap under the trees. Then, one day, the gates that divided their enclosures were left open forever. They would never be lonely again.

After the rescue
Bella & Simba

Lilongwe, Malawi

The sun sunk low over the bald red hills, catching the feathers of the circling and swooping kites. It had been another scorching summer's day in Malawi. All was quiet, except for the piping cries of the gray hornbills.

Lying in their favorite spot under a Baobab tree heavy with yellow fruit, and listening to the birds, were two lions: Bella, the one-eyed lioness and her mate, the magnificent, dark-maned Simba. Their healthy coats shone like gold in the rays of the setting sun.

Before the pair's watchful eyes, a porcupine scurried by. A few months ago, Simba might have made a grab for it and paid a hefty price. In the wild, without vets to lend a healing hand, the sharp, steel-hard quills of a porcupine can get stuck in a lion's jaw for life, making these little animals one of the lion's natural enemies. Like his mate, though, Simba had learned a lot since arriving at Lilongwe. He knew the plants and animals in his territory very well, and he would never be foolish enough to snap at a porcupine. Though he had been born into captivity, and lived— like Bella—in the most desperate of circumstances, the wild lion had completely awakened in Simba. He was master of everything he surveyed. A proud, fierce mate for the grand old lioness who he would love and protect for as long as she lived.

As the sun dipped below the horizon, Simba snuggled up to Bella and nuzzled her neck with his nose. The scent of lemon grass and wild orchids filled the air and, as the first stars of the African night blinked and sparkled, the two happy lions turned their heads, and roared into the velvet sky.

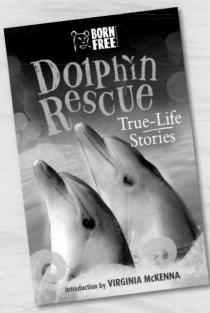

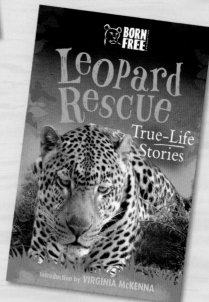

Read all the
rescue stories

Keep Wildlife in the Wild